This
Windfall

is for Pat, with thanks for all
your help, and much love to
you and to your beautiful
poems.

Maggie-of-the-Group
May 2000

Pitt Poetry Series

Ed Ochester, Editor

Windfall

New and Selected Poems

Maggie Anderson

Maggie Anderson

UNIVERSITY OF PITTSBURGH PRESS

Published by the University of Pittsburgh Press, Pittsburgh, Pa., 15261
Copyright © 2000, Maggie Anderson
Manufactured in the United States of America
Printed on acid-free paper
10 9 8 7 6 5 4 3 2 1

The publication of this book is supported by grants from
the Pennsylvania Council on the Arts and
the National Endowment for the Arts

Contents

I

from *Years That Answer*

Body and Soul

I have waited for this storm
as if for the one great love of my life
and meet it now knowing
I have always been ready.
Ripe to be licked by wind
I give it my own white back
like the leaves, toss in my mind
as the fireflies circle.
My arms edge toward it in twilight
with a tenderness I've sought
for years, my fingers slide familiar
over thin notes as if remembered.
Yes, this was how it would be:
all the houses and the sheds would pall
the air would fill and the sky yellow
before the breaking loose with it at last.
Just as my own precise rhythms
now rest one beat, then syncopate.
Just as that solid breath now blows
straight from the sax of the rain.

Caving

for Bill Matthews

who taught me: when you're afraid,
always lead.
So I quiver in, slithering
way out in front of everyone else,
the length of a football field
on my stupid belly without legs
dragging them behind like a knapsack.

When we can walk again, it's into rooms, they say,
as if this world underneath the limestone outcroppings
were someone's house

    walled with hanging bats
    murals of crumbly crickets
    the carpeted eyes of albino fish.

Where the stream dwindles
we suck breath into narrow passages,
up, through,
into more rooms, larger but the same
like the five hundred hats of Bartholomew Cubbins.
Until the waterfall: a roaring rush
going somewhere we cannot.

Some journeys have as their reason:
coming back.
Through crevices again, hopping along
like sideways monkeys.
Back through the water, and under it,
barking and glubbing like seals.
Back under the stalactites (hold tight to the ceiling)
dripping slow holes through our hats
to our heads.

Every rock looks like one we didn't pass
on the way in.
Once every trip, we turn off the lights
and pretend we're blind.
Pushing yellow-lighted hats before us
nostrils flaring with the wet
steely smell of carbide,
we haul ourselves on our elbows
toward the dim crack
we think is home. Famously wet and muddy we snivel out.
Sunshine and the world still there!
We take it all in: touch, remember.
It's not ready for us, the world.
We roll in the grass like dogs to get the muck off,
eat the flowers, fondle the tree bark,
shed dank bandages,
kneel in the weeds,
breathe.

What Grief Does

Like the ivy in my bedroom that climbs steadily from the red pot out the window, grief is the power of certain madness. And one dreams of bodies. They rise up from beneath blue blankets and expose themselves. They fly under the fluorescent lights and grow long fingernails; they never speak. The language of grief is silence.

This will never go away. It is your middle name; how you hate it. Grief grows with you, against you, forever; a movie title you can almost remember, or a friend's phone number. Like the ham bone from the party that the black dog buries and reburies under the forsythia bush, grief only becomes more yellow, a bright fire at the center of the earth. And it keeps showing up, again and again, on the living room floor.

The Keener

Because she came to hate
the short quick breaths of small people,
the whistling breathing of people with long noses,
and the harsh irregular snores of sleeping breathers,
she turned to grief as a true vocation.
Now she sits long nights with the dead
who never breathe.

She fondles her beads, the woman who loathes
the breathing of others, and the sound
she doesn't own rises above her body
like a balloon. She hears it
from the outside: a low moaning at first,
then a higher pitch, at last
a shrill and glistening wail.
In lamentation, she moves through the room,
it is her calling, howls numbly
at the body: *Your soul is loose now*
over the fields. It is sailing.
I can see it,
breathless, aloft.

The candles have been lit.
There is no sound of breathing but her own
and this is a perfect privacy.
The keener sits at ease in a hard chair.
She watches the dead man
in his white pine nightgown, in his coffin,
the intractable walls of it.

For the Anniversary of My Father's Death

Today is the last time I shall speak to you.
Now I shall cease speaking to you, my relative.
—from a Fox Indian chant to the dead

It has been one year. The wood on your casket must have started to decay. There is a stone at the head of your grave for safe passage of your soul and poinsettias from my uncle, your brother, who wishes you that.

You, dead, in your blue suit, on a mattress and pillow, with those brown spots on your hands, around your mouth and eyes. You are harder to see now. Someone else lives in your house.

But I can still see large plates with birds on them. They are arranged around a table, with a brown lace tablecloth, waiting for friends to arrive. There will be a party. And I can see sweat stains on a brown chair, a red bathrobe, two red pencils on a formica tabletop, three blue candles, a pile of newspapers, a black umbrella. Still, I tell you, my father, I will not die yet.

This new year will begin with my hands steady; the energy begins in my feet. There is a wheel above my left eye that has started to turn again. I will speak. This is the first song; this is the last song. This is the last song for you.

2

REFLECTIONS IN MY MIND

The fox faces east and has long ears.
Something curved with a tail follows him
or calls him back.
The fox begins to move.
He has left the one with a tail.
He is alone, pacing.
As he moves down the shelves, he grows longer
until at last the whole is full of fox,
russet, and heading east
and west at the same time.

And this same fox is sometimes green,
bent to graze like a horse.
An animal with two heads observes him.
They are at the top of a stack of drawers,
a spool of thread in each one.
The last drawer down is warped and won't close.
Beneath it is a small animal with bright eyes
and soft fur. It has a keen sense of smell
and supports all the mouths of the drawers
like gaping whales on its back
as if they were piled saddles,
creaking with thick, black leather.

4

OWL WITH YOUNG

Her watchful eyes like onions
sit in a fur circle that seems to be a halo
around her face.
Four smooth tail feathers
ride behind her like propeller blades.
She's always on the run.

The little owls surround her.
A plump one, soft as a duck,
steps on his brother's whooing head.
The baby girl owl seems to be reading the snow.
Her mother's face is as calm as the sun.

Some time ago the owl mother was always alone
in the wound branches over Baffin Island.
Now she no longer has time to huddle
in the trees, perfecting her deep tunes,
licking warmth to her feathers with a tiny tongue.

Only this blue seal over her left shoulder
still remembers those songs. He has always
been with her, with his strange beak. At night,
he drapes his flippers round her and soothes her,
tells her, you're the only one.

8

COMPLEX OF BIRDS

It's been snowing for days.
Everything connects,
a joining together like molecules of fish:
the hunter's hand to the mouth of the fox,
the fox to the bird's wing,
the small birds to each other,
and teeth in the beak in the leg
of the woman who stands with a seal on her arm.

Nothing is divided in this landscape.
Even the stones embrace.
A circle of feathers pivots
like the wrist of a wringing hand.
So no one will give up.
This is the only design possible
lavishly to protect us from harm.
It's been snowing for days.

Daphne

1

Daphne's in love again
round as a bracelet, loose as pajamas
eyes flashing real cool in her clothes.

Eyes across rooms, Daphne quivers,
smile too broad, she worries.

Am I obvious? Should I drop something?

Daphne's new lover leans across the table,
"Are you Catholic too?"

"God yes," Daphne sighs, "I'll be at your house at eleven."

2

Daphne studies her lover's face.

Eyes, nose, a few wrinkles.
Here's a spot like a seashell.

"You need something I can't give you,"
the lover says smiling.

Lacking, Daphne shudders. What could it be?
What could it be?
She swoons at her lover, "I'm sorry, I'm sorry."

3

Daphne thinks she has a secret.
No one knows. Daphne's special.

If I just hold perfectly still, not breathing,
fondle it like a stone. If I just contain it in . . .

But her lover's looking across fields,
eyes fixed on Daphne alone.

Somebody's run off with all of Daphne's secrets again.
Bereft, she remembers birds, falls to her lover, stutters.

4

Daphne is distracted.

Twitch.

I came here in a boat didn't I? Or was it a plane?
Let's see now. There were seats. I remember seats.
Some other passengers. A sort of little driver.
Somebody got drunk I think. Or was that yesterday?
And there was a throttle of some kind. I'm sure of it.

Briefly, just for a second,
Daphne forgets her name.

5

How she is called:
Through summer dusky streets from two blocks down:
        "Daphneee . . . Daphneee . . ."

In sleep, waking from nightmares:
        "Easy girl. Sh, sh, Daphne, you're ok."

Or from her sister at breakfast:
        "Daphne, you're really screwed up, y'know it?"

Or her lover:
        "I like how your shoulders move, Daphne. Daphne your
        body."

6

Lithe as a parakeet, Daphne swoops through the room.

Someone has a pillow on his head
so Daphne can't land there.
Puzzled, she returns to the cage, perches, contrite
does her one and only little number:

"Chirk, pretty boy. Chirk, pretty boy."

7

She is quieted. For no good reason.
Her lover returns to say it:

"I'll be everything for you, rest easy. Always. Always."

Daphne sighs, perfected she fades into cotton.

8

A latch clicks and Daphne's waiting.

Daphne's a vegetable.
Lying full in broad warm fields, she cries:

Cabbage plants and bean sprouts,
peas and cucumbers.

Daphne, daughter of tomato stakes,
you've done it again.

Lying there so clean and glistening
here it comes,
that same old harvester's smooth, dark hands.

Dancing in the Evening Sun

How my dad would whirl
my mother in it
wrapped in the Big Bands
they'd swing
her skirt flushed as a dahlia.

And then he'd dance me too,
toasting Mama on the curves.
On the tops of his slick black shoes
I'd scream at the dips.

Same sun that summer
we tagged dark Baltic waves
sand to our knees we swayed
in harbor lights and laughter.
Schnapps, to the sailors, the boats,
the horizon.

In the country the sun sinks
as the moon rises, and we edge the porch
slow drifting and gazing at ridges.
There's a racket of crickets,
someone with a banjo, then
the singing begins.

Or now,
I can see it slipping through trees.
I'm alone and elaborately
on my feet, moving
with some crazy song from the fifties,
a drink in my hand, I am exquisite.
Doing what needs doing,
I'm dancing alone
in this warm and brassy
evening sun going down.

II

from *Cold Comfort*

Country Wisdoms

Rescue the drowning and tie your shoe-strings.
—Thoreau, *Walden*

Out here where the crows turn around
where the ground muds over and the snow fences bend
we've been bearing up. Although

a green winter means a green graveyard
and we've buried someone every month since autumn
warm weather pulls us into summer by the thumbnails.

They say these things.

When the April rains hurl ice chunks onto the banks
the river later rises to retrieve them.
They tell how the fierce wind from the South

blows branches down, power lines and houses
but always brings the trees to bud.
Fog in January, frost in May

threads of cloud, they say, rain needles.
My mother would urge, be careful what you want,
you will surely get it.

More ways than one to skin that cat.
Then they say, Boot straps.
Pull yourself up.

House and Graveyard, Rowlesburg, West Virginia, 1935

I can't look long at this picture, a Walker Evans photograph
of a West Virginia graveyard in the Great Depression,
interesting for the sharp light it throws
on poverty, intimate for me because it focuses
on my private and familial dead. This is where

my grandparents, my Uncle Adrian and my Aunt Margaret
I am named for are buried. Adrian died at seven, long
before I was born. Margaret died in childbirth in 1929.
The morning sun falls flat against the tombstones
then spreads across Cannon Hill behind them. I see

how beautiful this is even though everyone was poor,
but in Rowlesburg nothing's changed. Everything
is still the same, just grayer. Beside the graveyard
is Fike's house with the rusty bucket, the tattered
trellis and the same rocker Evans liked. Miss Funk,

the school teacher, now retired, and her widowed sister
still live down the road out of the camera's range.
I remember how my Aunt Nita loved that mountain,
how my father told of swinging from the railroad
bridge down into the Cheat. Nita worked

for the Farm Security Administration too, as Evans did.
She checked people's houses for canned goods, to see
how many they had stored, and she walked the road
by here, every day. I can't look long at this picture.
It warps my history into politics, makes art
of my biography through someone else's eyes.
It's a good photograph, but Walker Evans
didn't know my family, nor the distance
his careful composition makes me feel now
from my silent people in their graves.

Independence Day, Terra Alta,
West Virginia, 1935

Maple trees rise around the picnic tables
as if an extension of the crowd. The young man
in the white linen suit and cap imagines himself
more dapper, and the girls selling kisses
under the striped canopy bend their heads.
Another girl, in a middy blouse with a party hat
tilted on her head, snarls at Walker Evans.
She doesn't want her picture made beside her mother
who is wearing a cloth coat with a fur collar
in early July, with the heat washing the fairgrounds
and everyone she knows standing around. She knows
what Evans doesn't: the talk behind the chance booth,
the way every gesture falls on her in a long shadow
of judgment and kin, her small mother in her stupid
cloth coat, clutching her purse to her bosom.

Mining Camp Residents,
West Virginia, 1935

They had to seize something in the face of the camera.
The woman's hand touches her throat as if feeling
for a necklace that isn't there. The man buries one hand
in his overall pocket, loops the other through a strap,
and the child twirls a strand of her hair as she hunkers
in the dirt at their feet. Maybe Evans asked them to stand
in that little group in the doorway, a perfect triangle
of people in the morning sun. Perhaps he asked them
to hold their arms that way, or bend their heads. It was
his composition after all. And they did what he said.

Spitting in the Leaves

In Spanishburg there are boys in tight jeans,
mud on their cowboy boots and they wear huge hats
with feathers, skunk feathers they tell me.
They do not want to be in school, but are.
Some teacher cared enough to hold them. Unlike
their thin disheveled cousins, the boys on Matoaka's
Main Street in October who loll against parking meters
and spit into the leaves. Because of them, someone
will think we need a war, will think the best solution
would be for them to take their hats and feathers,
their good country manners and drag them off somewhere,
to Vietnam, to El Salvador. And they'll go.
They'll go from West Virginia, from hills and back roads
that twist like politics through trees, and they'll fight,
not because they know what for but because what they know
is how to fight. What they know is feathers,
their strong skinny arms, their spitting
in the leaves.

Related to the Sky

At dusk, the blue line of these hills looks,
of course, like waves. So I wave. Hello hills.
Being hills, they do not speak back but just
draw in more light. Clouds, a small platoon
of healing hands, brush the trees. I try to find
the exact spot of the stars I liked in last night's
sky. Impossible. The leaves sift and muffle,
make room for the moon. I try to remember the color
of those leaves, how they were. Their shaggy
shapes, now draped in dark, cover the round animal
back of the hills. I try to remember how it was
once ocean floor and will be again, ancestral
and related to the sky.

The Wash in My Grandmother's Arms

In the only photograph of my paternal grandmother
she wears an apron and a dust cap, holds
her washing in her arms and squints at the camera
as if she finds photography too theoretical,
its attempt to capture history as it's made.
I never knew my grandmother but I've heard stories:
how she never wanted anyone to marry, how she feared
thunderstorms and the whistles as helper trains
pushed forty times their weight up Laurel Mountain.
My grandmother had seven children, no teeth,
and no belief in medicine. I recognize my relative
by her suspicion of impropriety in taking pictures.

It's my grandmother's conviction that, like lightning
or heavy trains on mountain sides working against
gravity, photography and marriage leave too much
to chance, to interpretation later of expression
or disaster. She is clearly overworked and resists
this fixing of the present in a beautiful nostalgia,
the diurnal translated as the representative.
My grandmother clutches her wash in the wind
and I locate my inheritance: how she holds to her task
in the face of speculation, as if the picture could
not possibly turn out, as if the sheets were trying
to fly away from her like pale extinct birds.

Cemetery, Saint Josephs Settlement

Having slept here and awakened among tombstones
and yellow fields, I feel affection for the Germans
who found this place over a century ago and stopped,
preferring to look down on the Ohio River forever
than to cross it. Some of them were born in German
and died in English: *geboren* 1848, died 1869
and none of them lived long. I walk past faded
granite Stations of the Cross and think of those
who've stayed, the descendants who live here now
in clean white houses. My connection to these people,
having slept an afternoon in full sun among their dead
seems as deep as my connection to you after ten years.
I know the concealed bones of these Germans now
as I know your back in sleep, and this lush grass feels
familiar as your hair. This is the intimacy history
allows: to find a beautiful place and to remain there.
This is the embrace of ambiguity that says, as these
people must have to each other before they fixed
the rafters for the barns, Yes, that's the Ohio
and beyond it, the West, but here we choose
to stop and make our settlement. Here, we will
build our houses, care for the children, educate
ourselves and bury what dies, among us.

With Wine

Es war nicht in mir. Es ging aus und ein.
Da wollt ich es halten. Da hielt es der Wein.
—Rilke, "Das Lied des Trinkers"

Now it is October, after harvest, and the fields fill up
with leaves and heavy rain. Someone has left our company
tonight and gone out to the dark pine forest where she
will drink alone in the rain. I do not want to laugh
at her as some do, speculating indiscreetly around
the dinner table, nor will I go out after her tonight
as the kind man putting on his jacket says he wants to.

I have been out there so many times myself,
because something frightened me in what passed by
as witty talk, because I heard again the imaginary
friends, calling from my childhood in the voices
no one ever could believe, calling with cold comfort
in the wine. Or I have gone because I know it is a time
of war, or nearly war, and there is nothing I can do.

I have run, as she will, from those who called me
to come back. I have staggered out to sit alone
on mossy rocks with wine and study the divisions
in branches of the trees, too sensible they seemed
to me, uninteresting, like pleats I hadn't planned on
in the sky, even though I might invent them into stars.

It is always nearly time of war. Tonight, because
I know she's out there, I don't have to be. She does
our work alone as I sit warm and calm beside the fire,
certain she is busy, following the blur of pines
out into the fields, tracking down our burdens:
everything that holds us and what we lose with wine,
what we think we have to gather in all by ourselves.

The Thing You Must Remember

The thing you must remember is how, as a child,
you worked hours in the art room, the teacher's
hands over yours, molding the little clay dog.
You must remember, how nothing mattered
but the imagined dog's fur, the shape of his ears
and his paws. The gray clay felt dangerous,
your small hands were pressing what you couldn't
say with your limited words. When the dog's back
stiffened, then cracked to white shards
in the kiln, you learned how the beautiful
suffers from too much attention, how clumsy
a single vision can grow, and fragile
with trying too hard. The thing you must
remember is the art teacher's capable
hands: large, rough and grainy,
over yours, holding on.

In My Mother's House

In the dream she is never sick and it is
always summer. She wears a polished cotton
sundress with wide shoulder straps, sits calmly
in a wooden lawn chair, green, I remember

from a photograph. I wonder if she'll know me
now, but want to keep formality awhile. I shake
her hand and introduce her to my friends,
who seem more like my parents' friends than mine,

subdued, and gathering with wine glasses
on the grass. Then I'm in the house my mother's
lived in since her death and she has changed
her clothes, put on her plaid viyella shirt.

She's sitting in her attic, among suitcases
and webs of boxes. A yellow triangle of light
skims the floor into the lap of her wool skirt.
I have had to be resourceful to get to her,

climbing up a bright blue ladder to the window
that broke down as I came through, transformed
itself from glass back into sand. My mother
holds a glass jar in her hands. She seems

preoccupied, as if it's tiring to be dead.
I ask her, *Are you weary?* and she says, *No,
are you? Yes,* I say and move into her arms
for a minute only, then she says she must
be off, something pressing, like the weight

on my heart as I wake, alive now, but her body
with me still, and warm, in the silk stockings
without shoes they dressed her in for burying.

In Singing Weather

Nature is a Haunted House—but Art—a House that
tries to be haunted.

—Emily Dickinson, letter to
  Thomas Wentworth Higginson, 1876

1

In September, third quarter moon
andante over first frost and that screech owl
is back again all night in the woods
below my house. Stray weeds
shift, directionless,
left too long alone.

Something's too rigid in this weather
as if it doesn't believe in itself
like the posturings of my own mind at twenty,
rushing at the delicacy I would have embraced.
And yet each thing connects to every other,

especially in memory we rely on these links,
contrapuntal: the hinge on the high school door
connects to my red hat, or to the warm brass
bracelets wrapping an arm I once caressed.
My dead parents, standing hand in hand
on a trellised porch, come back

with the evening sun. The September breeze
is a mannered piano, holding nothing
full-bodied or building for storm,
only each thing poised without words
against every other, the echo
of that screech owl, back.

2

In Indian Summer we know
the cold days have been only a trick
the weather plays in early autumn.
Like the dog at the screen door
wanting in, the heat is back now
in the afternoons, the summer holding.

In my garden, the wet tomato vines
are heavy laden and persistent
as a bagpipe drone, a burden
to be dealt with. So I pick
tomatoes and preserve them. So much
to do this time of year

yet the garden manages
to bear fruit as it decays
and the music of this weather
is as resonant as first
desire, the summer holding
just a little longer.

3

When the wind of October rises up under doorways
lifting winter from the plains after just
one warm day in ten, it beats against my vision
of the future, another end: one more
finished summer of melted grainy afternoons.

The dogs run restless at my calling,
far to the next hilltop, awash in weather
and frenzied disobedience. Me too, if someone
would dare to call me from this wind, now pulling
rain, inexorably pulling winter.

Even a dignified music with trumpets
couldn't match this wind, and today it's not
music I want to hear but the howling, whining
through silhouetted leaves of the wind
giving song to the season, point

against point. Dogs barking from dark
line of hill and the mottled moon rising
through red and yellow leaves in early cold.
Nights like these the future takes hold, latching
onto the places we already understand it:

prescience knit to sentimentality. It's time now
to speak loudly and clearly and straight into the wind
from which the dogs at last turn back; noses to the dirt
they track my boot scent, eight quick paws crunching cornstalks,
four long ears whipping dust up into wind.

4

The light revolves in its own whimsy
largo through branches and falling leaves:
the hard blues now of shuffle and dip,
plunked banjo, fiddle wheeze and guitar.

All through the pale October dusk I have called out,
called out but made no sound. The hills, tucked
in red blankets of sun, are my voice for this weather,
my round cousins. When I can't sing, they lull the sky

and improvise limpid tunes for the barns.
My voice makes only faint and courtly gestures
toward the rim of light, off, there, another
scene I named badly, another collapse of words.

Even the dogs won't go out in this weather.
Tonight is not a night for walking but for sitting
still on the soft warm rugs of winter coming,
hard blues, and the laying in.

5

Perched on the kitchen table I look out
at morning fog so thick it muffles
even its own soft noise over white November
fields and does not burn off by noon

but goes on covering us all day. A year
has seemed a month or less, yet I find
I don't work harder, now I'm dying faster,
just pay more careful attention to the sky.

Nearly all the yellow leaves are gone
and those plants I hung to give green
this winter cover the whole window now
greener every day against white mist.

Fuga, from the Latin, *flight,* and in the long
rests I think I hear *glissando,* egregious
narrowing down to that raw muscle,
my heart, with its hum of longing.

Still, I am less grim in fog and bare trees
than in October with that crazy wind. Grandeur
makes me nervous, and now the ravaged ground
and shabby bean vines seem, at least, to match

my soul. Where there is congruence, there is
hope. After long silence, there might be music,
subtle and insistent as the Hudson River,
tidal, as far north as Troy.

6

At the winter solstice I know again
the only point is to catch the light,
the soft shading behind black branches
against white sky. I try to hold
this moment of change in the sun
the east lit up in negative,
the hills to the south glowing
from inside, and the dark sweep
where the leaves were carried off into clouds
or another range of hills. The point, after all,
is to say only: winter light, what's here.

The brown summer boxes of leaves thrown down
and abandoned are now resurrected in dirt,
in the vacancy under the curve of fence line,
in the deeper shadow where the road
lies hung in its ruts. I give rapt
attention to weather and record it:
the solid black trunks of the oaks,
the small evening fires.
A formal music comforts
by velocity of measure and thin melody
cello obbligato, the deep soft voice of coming snow.

7

Even the breathless dead seem,
sometimes, nevertheless, to sing.

At last it's snowed and hushed the hills,
all the forest veins revealed.

The December sky is generous once more
with a light tender as a ragtime piano

frowsy as the woman who plays it by ear
and tilts her head. She's hard as nails.

Her hands build bookcases and every ivory shelf thrums,
as she jumps all her tricky sweetness off the stool

and onto the floor. She sings in a frolic fast
as a running heart, each note wound to every other.

After long silence, there is music again,
thin lip of moon and again bright stars,

the weeds safe now in their coffins of ice,
in singing weather. The pets of my childhood

nose the white drifts in bright collars
and bows and I whistle them home to me,

in from the cold. Now the formal dead
can love me back, with their voices

carried on the wind. And I can hold them,
rock them in my own melodic arms.

Heart Fire

Three months since your young son shot himself
and, of course, no one knows why. It was October.
Maybe he was following the smell of dying leaves
or the warmth of the fire in the heart, so hard
to locate in a country always readying for war.

One afternoon we sat together on your floor, drinking
tea and listening to Brahms on the radio. He would
have liked this music, you told me. He would have liked
everything I like now and what he wouldn't like I don't
like either. He has made the whole world look like him.

Today, driving into Pittsburgh, I see you are right.
The sky is cold blue like a shirt I once saw him
wear and the bare trees are dark, like his hair.
I see how vulnerable the grasses are, pale and flimsy
by the roadsides, trying to stand straight in the wind.

At Canonsburg, all the pink and green and purple houses
have the same slant of roof toward the hill, like toys
because I'm thinking about children, how sometimes
we want to give them up if they seem odd and distant,
yet even if they die before us, we cannot let them go.

I see your son in landscapes as I drive, in a twist
of light behind a barn before the suburbs start,
or under a suburban street light where a tall boy
with a basketball has limbs like those he had just
outgrown. Because I want to think he's not alone

I invent for him a heart fire even the unenlightened
living are sometimes allowed to see. It burns past
the white fluorescence of the city, past the steel mills
working off and on as they tell us we need, or don't
need, heavy industry for fuel, or war. Your son

keeps me company, driving down the last hill into
Pittsburgh, in the tunnel as I push for good position
in the lanes. He is with me as I spot the shiny cables
of the bridge and gear down, as all the lights beyond
the river come on now, across his safe, perfected face.

Anything We Leave Forever

The hills stand in each other's shadows at dusk
and I stare off at them, stunned, the way I'd be
if, walking through a strange town one day,
I looked down and found all the smooth stones
I piled up so carefully and then abandoned
as a child. I want to say it's the contrast
that startles me: black limbs against flat sun.
It's not that, but how the day remains behind
the purple rim of light; how anything we leave
forever, in the grand way, returns to us
unsummoned and at last without remorse, in details
like the tracery of twigs here in this evening
light behind the trees. Five miles across the valley,
the gold reliquaries of the afternoon are stored:
spiny branches cupped by clouds, the finger bones
of saints clicking in the satchels of the sky.

III

from *A Space Filled with Moving*

Ontological

This is going to cost you.
If you really want to hear a
country fiddle, you have to listen
hard, high up in its twang and needle.
You can't be running off like this,
all knotted up with yearning,
following some train whistle,
can't hang onto anything that way.
When you're looking for what's lost
everything's a sign,
but you have to stay right up next to
the drawl and pull of the thing
you thought you wanted, had to
have it, could not live without it.
Honey, you will lose your beauty
and your handsome sweetie, this whine,
this agitation, the one you sent for
with your leather boots and your guitar.
The lonesome snag of barbed wire you have
wrapped around your heart is cash money,
honey, you will have to pay.

Empirical

Everything sad that ever happened to me
I have mourned beside a river.
This afternoon I sat by the bridge pilings
and studied the slow drawl of the Willamette
as it choked on the rocks and spit its current
back through the branches of cottonwoods.
Flood is easy for a river, like giving up.
What's hard is carving a valley, pulling
toward the sea on its hands and knees.

In my room there are twelve panes of glass
and beyond them a furnace of pink azaleas
pulling in the dark. It has been blue dusk
for some time now, and I have been watching
shadows alter these flowers to banked coals.

I lie down to wait for the river.
What I love about sorrow is its capacity
for metaphor, how sadness makes things
resemble each other. To the river, my body
is just a stone. I give it what I have,
first one, then the other of my empty hands.
It lifts and carries me a few feet
past blossoms of skunk cabbage, beautiful,
like sheaths of sun. I float for awhile
seeing clouds the way I saw them as a child.
My long hair trails behind me like a windsock
seining twigs and fish. At the bottom is
the vegetal mud, and it's not like anything
but it's mine. Like burning embers,

the azaleas suck up the dark earth
they fall to. I cloud the brown silk
of the river, and I take it in.

Marginal

This is where I live,
at the edge of this ploughed field
where sunlight catches meadow grasses
and turns them silver-yellow
like the tines of the birches
at the rim of the forest, where
lumps of earth are scabbed over
with rust colored pine needles
and one noisy crow has been
traversing them all morning.
Deep in these woods
his feathers have fallen so often
in some places they have started
to pile up like black snow.

I prefer it here, at the line
where the forest intersects
the field, where deer and groundhog
move back and forth to feed
and hide. On these juts and outcroppings
I can look both ways, moving
as that crow does, all gracelessness
and sway across the heaved-up fields,
then tricky flight between
the overhanging branches he somehow
manages never to scrape against.
This life is not easy,
but wings mix up with leaves here,
like the moment when surf turns into

undertow or breaker, and I can
poise myself and hold
for a long time, profoundly
neither one place nor another.

Anywhere But Here

Memory's got its suitcase packed and is always leaving
whatever's right in front of it, the present moment,
which now holds pleated yellow dahlias
brushing my kitchen windowsill.
They look bewildered, like tourists,
mapping out rest stops and bending their heavy heads.
Last September I was a tourist myself,
bewildered and resting my feet
beside a souvenir vendor in black beret and undershirt
in Piazza San Marco, watching the pigeons pacing
the roof of the Ducal Palace and the ubiquitous tourists
lining up for gondola rides, while I waited for
a British tour guide to lead me out of Venice.
When a Greek steamer pulled into the basin
and announced itself, the pigeons whirred and lifted,
the tourists quieted their hundred languages,
and in the steamy lull that followed
the bells in the campanile sounded so American,
clanging with the ship horn like wind chimes
and traffic scored for pump organ, that I suddenly
remembered how, back home in Pennsylvania,
my dahlias would be blooming all alone where
I had planted them in the warm spring ground.
That was only homesickness, the sweet exile
of travel, but what shall I call this pang
I feel now as I reach out to touch plush petals
here in my own back yard, heavy
and golden as Venetian evening sunlight
on marble bridges, leading me back
to green water, over water,
past the *fondamenta*'s little barber poles

of piers, below balconies with louvered windows
opened into rooms with parquet floors
and who knows what other splendors?

Heart Labor

When I work too hard and then lie down,
even my sleep is sad and all worn out.
You want me to name the specific sorrows?
They do not matter. You have your own.
Most of the people in the world
go out to work, day after day,
with their voices chained in their throats.
I am swimming a narrow, swift river.
Upstream, the clouds have already darkened
and deep blue holes I cannot see
churn up under the smooth flat rocks.
The Greeks have a word, *paropono,*
for the complaint without answer,
for how the heart labors, while
all the time our faces appear calm
enough to float through in the moonlight.

Sonnet for Her Labor

My Aunt Nita's kitchen was immaculate and dark,
and she was always bending to the sink
below the window where the shadows off the bulk
of Laurel Mountain rose up to the brink
of all the sky she saw from there. She clattered
pots on countertops wiped clean of coal dust,
fixed three meals a day, fried meat, mixed batter
for buckwheat cakes, hauled water, in what seemed lust
for labor. One March evening, after cleaning,
she lay down to rest and died. I can see Uncle Ed,
his fingers twined at his plate for the blessing;
my Uncle Craig leaning back, silent in red
galluses. No one said a word to her. All that food
and cleanliness. No one ever told her it was good.

Holding the Family Together

Near midnight, driving a sliver of backcountry road
between two steel cities, I remember the article
I read last week about the awful things that happen
to women out after dark in cars. Outside is only
forest and frozen creek bed, patches of black ice
on the highway, and "safety" has become
the soft melding of gears I'm counting on
to get me home. Thirty years ago, "home"
was only my father and I, eating our meals
in silence by the radio. I was as frightened then
as the small animals, whose eyes shine beside the road
my headlights illuminate, then flood with dark,
in a time so fast they cannot comprehend it.
My father said he was "holding the family together,"
the way Edith Piaf, singing now on the radio,
holds a song together through marching band music,
carousel rhythms, an abrupt modulation to a minor key.
C'était pas moi, I sing along, trying to make the dark
companionable, as I hit a pothole and command my tires
not to blow out here. If I needed help and if
it came, it would be another thing to fear,
like the knife blades my father
flashed through the yellow kitchen,
saying, *These, you see, could kill us both.*
Nothing to be afraid of, I lied to myself
until he would quiet and tell me, *Listen
to the music.* Piaf's still singing
but I've gone rigid now with defense,
trusting to the wheel bearings and accelerator cable,
holding the family together, in my familiar
numb pantomime of a landscape, in which
no enemy could recognize me as his prey.

Long Story

To speak in a flat voice
Is all that I can do.
—James Wright, "Speak"

I need to tell you that I live in a small town
in West Virginia you would not know about.
It is one of the places I think of as home.
When I go for a walk, I take my basset hound
whose sad eyes and ungainliness always draw
a crowd of children. She tolerates anything
that seems to be affection, so she lets the kids
put scarves and ski caps on her head
until she starts to resemble the women who have to dress
from rummage sales in poverty's mismatched polyester.

The dog and I trail the creek bank with the kids,
past clapboard row houses with Christmas seals
pasted to the windows as a decoration.
Inside, television glows around the vinyl chairs
and curled linoleum, and we watch someone old
perambulating to the kitchen on a shiny walker.
Up the hill in town, two stores have been
boarded up beside the youth center and miners
with amputated limbs are loitering outside
the Heart and Hand. They wear Cat diesel caps
and spit into the street. The wind
carries on, whining through the alleys,
rustling down the sidewalks, agitating
leaves, and circling the courthouse steps
past the toothless Field sisters who lean
against the flagpole holding paper bags
of chestnuts they bring to town to sell.

History is one long story of what happened to us,
and its rhythms are local dialect and anecdote.
In West Virginia a good story takes awhile,
and if it has people in it, you have to swear
that it is true. I tell the kids the one about
my Uncle Craig who saw the mountain move
so quickly and so certainly it made the sun
stand in a different aspect to his little town
until it rearranged itself and settled down again.
This was his favorite story. When he got old,
he mixed it up with baseball games, his shift boss
pushing scabs through a picket line, the Masons
in white aprons at a funeral, but he remembered
everything that ever happened, and he knew how far
he lived from anywhere you would have heard of.

Anything that happens here has a lot of versions,
how to get from here to Logan twenty different ways.
The kids tell me convoluted country stories
full of snuff and bracken, about how long
they sat quiet in the deer blind with their fathers
waiting for the ten-point buck that got away.
They like to talk about the weather,
how the wind we're walking in means rain,
how the flood pushed cattle fifteen miles downriver.

These kids know mines like they know hound dogs
and how the sirens blow when something's wrong.
They know the blast, and the stories, how
the grown-ups drop whatever they are doing
to get out there. Story is shaped
by sound, and it structures what we know.
They told me this, and three of them
swore it was true, so I'll tell you
even though I know you do not know
this place, or how tight and dark the hills
pull in around the river and the railroad.

I'll say it as the children spoke it,
in the flat voice of my people:
down in Boone County, they sealed up
forty miners in a fire. The men who had come
to help tried and tried to get down to them,
but it was a big fire and there was danger,
so they had to turn around
and shovel them back in. All night long
they stood outside with useless picks and axes
in their hands, just staring at the drift mouth.
Here's the thing: what the sound must have been,
all those fire trucks and ambulances, the sirens,
and the women crying and screaming out
the names of their buried ones, who must have
called back up to them from deep inside
the burning mountain, right up to the end.

Closed Mill

I'm not going to tell you everything,
like where I live and who I live with.
There are those for whom this would be
important, and once perhaps it was to me,
but I've walked through too many lives
this year, different from my own,
for a thing like that to matter much.
All you need to know
is that one rainy April afternoon,
exhausted from teaching six classes
of junior high school students,
I sat in my car at the top of a steep hill
in McKeesport, Pennsylvania, and stared
for a long time at the closed mill.

"Death to Privilege," said Andrew Carnegie,
and then he opened up some libraries,
so that he might "repay his deep debt,"
so that light might shine on Pittsburgh's poor
and on the workers in the McKeesport Mill.
The huge scrap metal piles below me
pull light through the fog on the river
and take it in to rust in the rain.
Many of the children I taught today
were hungry. The strong men who are
their fathers hang out in the bar
across the street from the locked gates
of the mill, just as if they were still
laborers with lunch pails, released
weary and dirty at the shift change.

Suppose you were one of them?
Suppose, after twenty or thirty years,
you had no place to go all day
and no earned sleep to sink down into?
Most likely you would be there too,
drinking one beer after another,
talking politics with the bartender,
and at the end of the day
you'd go home, just as if you had
a paycheck, your body singing
with the pull and heave of imagined
machinery and heat. You'd talk mean
to your wife who would talk mean back,
your kids growing impatient and arbitrary,
way out of line. Who's to say you would not
become your father's image, the way any of us
assumes accidental gestures,
a tilt of the head, hard labor,
or the back of his hand.

From here the twisted lines of wire
make intricate cross-hatchings against
the sky, gray above the dark razed mill's red
pipe and yellow coals, silver coils of metal
heaped up and abandoned. Wall by wall,
they are tearing this structure down.
Probably we are not going to say
too much about it, having as we do
this beautiful reserve, like roses.

I'll say that those kids were hungry.
I would not dare to say the mill won't
open up again, as the men believe.
You will believe whatever you want to.
Once, philanthropy swept across our dying cities
like industrial smoke, and we took everything
it left and we were grateful, for art
and books, for work when we could get it.
Any minute now, the big doors buried under
scrap piles and the slag along this river
might just bang open and let us back inside
the steamy furnace that swallows us
and spits us out like food, or heat
that keeps us warm and quiet
inside our little cars in the rain.

Abandoned Farm, Central Pennsylvania

In the middle of my life,
orphaned, childless,
I am perched on a promontory
of genealogy, where branches
fade from the yellowed pages
and the farm goes back to the wild
where it came from.

I had always thought I'd come on this
the other way, from across the open fields,
the long approach to distant house and barn
sheltered by a grove of trees. Instead,
I have stumbled out of woodland
up against a vine-covered back porch
where twisted limbs of hickory and maple
are knocking back the eaves.
This was a good house:
wide-planked floors and hand-hewn timbers,
mortised and pegged in place,
and what's left of it is good house still,
the uprights plumb.

This farm is no one's property,
no one claims it, sees it
as kin do, through the eyes of the community.
Beyond the smear of wavy glass
is kitchen: dry midden piled
on the ample hearth, a table leaning
against the wall. I can lift that table
up in my mind and see them eating.
I can people my vision

and watch them in the fidget of their tasks,
but I cannot make them speak to me
beyond the harsh monosyllables of tools
and work: *seeds, plough, cash,* and *crock;*
sons, and *wood,* and *hoe.*

⋀⋀⋁

The kitchen garden fences in
a stingy crop of blackberries between pickets.
Chamomile and dill still volunteer
among the wild mullein and cinquefoil.
This garden has become its own
ripe compost, fitted
like a bird's nest to its set of feathers.
Here is everything it needs:
mulch, and loam, and seeds sowed
by birds and wind to sprout at random.
Whatever grows is harvested
by groundhog and deer.

A shadow path leads to the ground cellar
where the dark smells like apples,
mildew, and potatoes. A mud-caked boot still
tramples down the reeds of broken baskets.
In this sarcophagus of thrift and dream,
a few cloudy Mason jars have exploded.
Glass shards stick to the moss,
and sweet preserves have splattered
on the door like clotted blood.

⋀⋀⋁

One year I thought I would visit
all the family graves and carry flowers,
tidy them like they used to do
on Decoration Day. I started
with my mother's family, weeding out
around the big granite headstone,
pulling ivy and pokeweed back
from my grandparents' chiseled names.
I swept, and placed wildflowers across
the mounds of dirt, telling myself I was
doing my duty to the dead.
But standing alone, the only living DeLancy
in the graveyard, I felt how outnumbered
I am by my kin on the other side,
the only one not yet come to the table.

I drove to where my parents lie
side by side in a modern cemetery.
Their graves are kept clean
with perpetual care, so there was nothing
for me to do. I sat down on top of one,
then the other. I wanted to see:
skulls and teeth, and water
pooling up in the wormy satin
of the boxes they were laid in.
I wanted to touch their hip sockets
and metatarsals, search out strands of hair
or threads of cloth. I am now
ten years younger than my mother was
when she died. I wanted to see

if time goes this fast under the ground,
if I could locate some trace of face
that looks like mine on my mother's bones.

~~~

Beyond the house the garden path widens out
to cattle road and gravel,
to the wide gabled doors of the banked barn
built into the hillside.
I had not imagined it so large,
nor the air so still, the floor
cluttered with pitchforks
and wheelbarrows, feed pails,
bedsprings, snakes of rotten rope.
In the regimented light
from vent slits shaped like sheaves of wheat,
I can see fine workings
of white oak beams, and a loft
of piled locust, cut and saved
for fence rail and door peg
and never used.

In my own house are the books and dishes,
the photographs, and cuff links in small boxes
lined with velvet willed to me by my family.
I worry who to leave them to.
Even sentiment wants function,
and some of these once-loved objects
have no more use, even to me,
than the tidy stalls below,
releasing their sweet stink

of moldy provender and stony dung
from the astringent masonry.

Barn swallows stir, racket out
from the thatchings of their nests.
A rusty rake rattles near my feet
with a curl and twist of black snake.
I freeze, then back out slowly,
the way I have learned to move warily
at the place where human habitation
has left off.

~~~

The scrubby meadow riffles with insect whir
and chicory. Maybe it was right
to have found the house and barn
before the fields, to see first
what passed for intimacy among this family.
Out here is what all the neighbors saw,
the public lap of their prosperity,
the bottomland of the Susquehanna River Valley,
rounded out into the elbows of the Alleghenies.
In the southwest corner, field stones
are piled against the windbreak.
An old potato digger leans, like a fussy child,
against crumpled wire fence.
I mount the sun-warmed grooves of seat
and lean onto the handles, just as if
I have known this movement all my life.

~~~

Who knows what the body can remember
from far back, through the blood
traces of habit and sweat?
In a little while I'm going home.
For now I feel at ease,
a hermit crab, assuming my regency
of atmosphere and paraphernalia.

The woods are going to take this home place
back one day. And the dark hills will keep on
pushing and kneading this fertile valley down
as the river rinses it. A family lived here
for generations, and they were preoccupied,
like the rest of us, with food and sleep,
the unpredictability of weather.
I'm as at home as any of us
likes to think we are,
in our saving up for later,
in the solitary repetitions of our labors.

Beyond Even This

Who would have thought the afterlife would
look so much like Ohio? A small town place,
thickly settled among deciduous trees.
I lived for what seemed a very short time.
Several things did not work out.
Casually almost, I became another one
of the departed, but I had never imagined
the tunnel of hot wind that pulls
the newly dead into the dry Midwest
and plants us like corn. I am
not alone, but I am restless.
There is such sorrow in these geese
flying over, trying to find a place to land
in the miles and miles of parking lots
that once were soft wetlands. They seem
as puzzled as I am about where to be.
Often they glide, in what I guess is
a consultation with each other,
getting their bearings, as I do when
I stare out my window and count up
what I see. It's not much really:
one buckeye tree, three white frame houses,
one evergreen, five piles of yellow leaves.
This is not enough for any heaven I had
dreamed, but I am taking the long view.
There must be a backcountry of the beyond,
beyond even this and farther out,
past the dark smoky city on the shore
of Lake Erie, through the landlocked passages
to the Great Sweetwater Seas.

The Invention of Pittsburgh

That was the year I drove around all the time
talking about poems. I'd eat my lunch in the car
between one public high school and another.
I was so exhausted, preoccupied with gearshifts
and poetry workshops. I forgot to pay
my income taxes and wandered around acting like
I was really earning what they were paying me.
That was the year Ed kept telling me
to eat more squid and, being accommodating,
I tried. I had to eat squid, gelatinous chalk dust,
in every Chinese restaurant in Philadelphia;
in New Hampshire, broiled squid, a double order,
no garnish, no rice. And once in Vermont,
I was so overwhelmed by the multifoliate
deciduous trees that I ordered a squid sandwich
in a health food restaurant on Lake Bomoseen
that came to me on whole wheat bread with sprouts.
Then I was in Eugene, on a Saturday in February,
about four o'clock. I asked for a bowl of squid
in a little restaurant on Polk Street
but what I got looked exactly like Pittsburgh,
or the Pittsburgh I suddenly knew that I,
a forty-year-old poet sitting in Oregon,
was about to invent from whimsy and weariness.
There were thirty bridges, and thirty highways
followed the rivers. Neighborhoods laced
the hillsides, through detours and freeway
construction around the inclines and concrete tubes,
circuiting the long walls of old mines buried under
the gray Carnegie libraries and the universities,
the closed mills and the steaming slag piles,

the orthodox churches on the North Side
where they bless the cabbages at Easter.
This is what the lonely imagination finds in
squid: the aftertaste of scallops, the texture
of cheap perfume, bright yellow leaves
on the sycamores in the parking lot
off Forbes, kids recumbent with radios
on the lawns of the robber barons' mansions,
intricate lingerie wadded up in a hotel sink
on the Boulevard of the Allies in Pittsburgh,
the tough, sweet city of the workers.

Big Romance

This spring my wildest love has been
the lilacs and the pink azaleas
blossoming in after dinner light
along the alleys. I love how
raindrops remain awhile
like pearls at the neckline
of the chemise of these geraniums,
and I dress up when I go out
to woo them with my dark hair
and my gentle hands. When I hold
this lavender and yellow-spotted
Korean rhododendron, it reminds me
of the open faces of healthy children
I have known, well-fed and clever,
in clean sneakers and little overalls.
I have totally surrendered to
the opulence of suburban shrubbery,
colors like the old hotels, magenta,
puce, red moon and orange of pumpkin pulp,
yellow of wild mustard, citronella.
Only the brightest ones draw bees,
but I am fickle and speak sweetly
even to the pale gardenias
throwing their cloying fragrance
indiscriminately over the warm air.
I would like to be a person they find
attractive, so I have gathered
all the fallen petals from the paths
and made a hat of them,
a hat I will wear like my heart
on my sleeve, foolish as I've grown
with love for flowers.

As Long As I Can

The tall red dahlias have arrived
like a crowd of Anabaptists
ready to expel the Lutherans
and burn up their bills and contracts.
All afternoon I've been outside
trying to invent their similes.
Sometimes they look like second graders,
flummoxed by the end of summer,
staked to their desks. Or rain-soaked
scarecrows, reduced to only hair
and a dark center of eye.
This has been the last warm day.
When I riffle through the petals of one
blossom the size of an infant's head,
I can see mortality's brown wound
already festering at the edges,
so I'm going to cut this one
and carry it inside with me
to watch it fade. I will coffin it
in the silver salver where it will
float on oily water, releasing the sweet
perfumes of its anarchic fire.

Wild Berries

The warm and uncut fields above the house
opened out in the afternoon
like yellow petals of loosestrife
as the jarflies fluttered
in the soft palaver of the breeze,
and I waded snakey meadow grass
to root out thickets
of wild black raspberries, tangled
among chokecherry and greenbrier.
The air cooled as I passed
into the woods and stood
in the flickering light above
little umbrellas of mayapples.
Two thin blackberry vines trailed
across the shifting stones
of the old smokehouse, and I ate three
handfuls, let a few more go, before
I crouched beneath the falling roof,
crossed under, and started down
the steep hillside's tarpaulin
of winter-soaked, rotten leaves.

Beneath the wide mittens
of sassafras, I caught the swift
propulsion of descent
in the crotches of hackberry
and beech, trapezing from branch
to branch of low-hanging maples, down
to the dry creek bed where I looked back
up at the cut and switch
of light through moving leaves.

I followed the murmur of water
up the neck of the hollow
to where the mountain's froth
churned against the rocks,
then pulled up the other side,
through oaks and lightning-struck
limbs of poplars, arm over arm,
clutching loose vines,
pushing my knuckles flat to the ground.

Where I hauled up, there was sunlight
on an old logging road, scarred
with tire ruts pooled like ponds
and shimmering with false morels
and fiddlehead ferns. The slash
of clear-cut timber was coming back
in fireweed, and waxy white
blossoms of mountain laurel melted
down the hillside to the trail.
I walked to where the sun fell
flat and hot on an upland clearing
where the grasses caught the sunlight
red, and the towhees teased at me
from the broken fence line. There,
I found no black raspberries, only
scratchy, overripe pellets of blackberries
already picked over by the birds.

I trudged back out the log road
down to the untrustworthy bridge
and followed the stream to where the blacktop

meets the farm road, where the filth,
new-cut from the berm, had been bedded
down in the creek's dry sluice. There,
beneath layers of dead sumac, dogbane,
limp columbine and pennyroyal,
were hundreds of black raspberry vines,
none yet discovered by the birds,
and in full ripeness.

With luck's greed I picked
until my fingers ached
from the precision of the movement
and the berries dropped one after another
into the coffee can. I bent and crawled,
then stumbled out, my hands splotched
with berry blood and brambles.
Then in the lighted kitchen,
I rolled the dough and stirred
the thick syrup. I poured the dark rain
of berries straight from the can
into the damp spread of the crust
and turned them with a wooden spoon.
I waited while the pie baked.
I waited while it cooled on the porch railing.
Then, in the white heavy air
of dew and evening, I ate.

Setting Out

Days like this I can't imagine death as
any more compelling than the man in the tollbooth
on the George Washington Bridge where, as a child,
I thought there was a lane for the dying
down which my mother chose to go, quietly accepting
her designated token and setting out
across the lighted necklace of the Hudson,
draped above its sludge and juts of pier.
My walk today was not this risky,
but maybe as theatrical, with September light
drawing in its purple sashes bit by bit
through the cutwork of the trees.
The sky held only cat-shaped and bosomy white clouds
like the ones children color, and I walked
the back road to the meadow, where I admired
the smattering of blue asters among daisies,
where two yellow Monarchs were doing dips
and quick dissolves. There was a bustle of travel,
in the jarflies circuiting the heated grasses,
the birds in rehearsal for departure, lining up
in parallelograms that lifted and then luffed
a silent V of backwashed wind. It was so quiet there
beside the brook, where the dog lay down with me,
relaxed as an old loafer in the sun,
which picked up the red in her fur and made
a kind of halo around her ears, so she seemed
a fallen angel dog, exhausted from chasing shadows
down the asphalt road. If I'm lucky
I still have quite a few more years to live.
The goldenrod was waving its cabled lures
in the breeze, and I thought of my father,

his weak hands waving from his hospital window
where he stood, a shabby weed. He was calling out
to me, and I was far below him, hurrying off
to be with you. How could we have been so crazy
in love in the midst of all that grief?
Most of my walk today was leisure and delight,
no more than the usual cleats of sorrow
attaching to my heart, but even the most beautiful
of late summer days can cramp into a memory, uneasy
attention to what we haven't thought about in years,
like the wrong mother's hand in the shopping line.
We hold it until we feel the strangeness, then
let go, a little frightened, a little embarrassed
to have done this thing, caught off balance,
like the quiet leafy path I just now turned to
and surprised myself by starting to walk down.

The Only Angel

I can see that, what with one thing and another,
you're all worn down, but you have to quit
calling out to me with all these elegies.
You're sweet, but it's clear you don't know shit
from shineola. I could bring you to your knees
with one hard kiss, but I want you to mother
up the good life, get around a little more.
You're trying too hard, hedging your bets.
I am not a porcelain light behind the trees.
You can't touch me. I'm not even here yet,
your heart attack, your wreck, your slow disease.
I am what you cannot know, the blank imposing door
that you will storm one day to get at me,
hot and ready, since you will have to be.

IV

New Poems

Knife

My memory honed to an edge,
this leaf, that bread, the narrative of
my father holding the blade to my throat.
What do you know about knives?
If I told you I have followed you home
at night, that I know your car,
the streets you travel, where you live,
and that I have waited for you evenings
after work with a knife in my hand,
if I told you this, would you be afraid,
stay awake, believe me?

The knife I always carry in my pocket was
meant to save me from you. Now it is
transformed and I am holding not a shield
but a sword, not protection but a weapon,
a sophisticated hunger to smell your fear.
I cannot tell if what I feel is

annoyance or horror,
this place where I got hurt by knives,
and by threat of them,
the place I want to give you in this poem
and let you wonder if I mean it,
if it is, as we say, really true.

Interior with Letter

Dear fat chair,
upholstered topiary,
your pillows are the size of cumulus clouds
tucked into horizon, and for months now
I have come to sit beside you.
I have come to lean my head on your arm,
to mumble and weep into your green lap.
Once you let me hit your side with my hot fist.
Once I ran away from you for no good reason:
fear of furniture. But now I've grown comfortable
enough with this conventional decor
and you are soft foliage to me,
rest for my weak leg and my shaky hands,
my unfurnished heart.

The Sleep Writer

Lovely afternoon. The firing squad.
Bottles lined up in the sun.
Dahlias. Men in uniform. Daffodils.
Children with satchels coming home from school.
I am writing in my sleep. The journey here
was not very long, only a little cold,
the fast horses of exhaustion pulled me.
Too many people, I write, *are watching*
what we do. Too much sun on the green glass.
The firing squad. The lovely afternoon.

Black Dog Remembers

Everything. No forgetfulness here:
the glare of concentration,
pathological vigilance. The growl-snarl
deep-in-the-throat-up-in-your-face
when anyone comes to the door.
Black dog took threats to heart: the knives,
the hiss and scent of the unvented gas heater,
the andiron and the penis, the fist.
Now I hold onto this big black dog
stretched across my chest, so close
it might smother me, or rescue
me from the other, mad dog,
dead dog, my father.

The Game

I take the black dog down
to the field in early morning.
I find a stick heavy enough
to seem like work, and thick
enough for her to get her teeth into.
We begin.
Sit, I tell her.
Fetch. Drop.
Sit, fetch, drop.
Black dog leaps and turns and slides
through wet grass and muck.
She wants to outrun the stick's trajectory,
to catch the task midair,
get ahead of the game.
So many sticks, so many ways
to chase and grab and bring.
Although she pants and shakes and slows,
black dog would do this unto death
if I did not stop her, which I always do,
by making the sticks go away,
by holding her wet, muddy head in my hands
to slip the leash back on, by wiping off
her bloody jaw. *Sit, black dog,*
I say. *Lie down. Lie down.*

Black Dog Lies Down

Rolling moss gathers on the stones
and the sky is thick with weather. *Oregon,*
a good place to have lived, I say now.
Past. Perfect. Tense. A good place to have
once been from. When I lie on my bed,
I listen to the ocean and look up
through a planetarium display of stars,
the northern constellations: Star. Cross.
Lovers. Big Bear. I'm tired of being afraid,
so for once I refuse it. It's only fear,
the carsick feeling that makes the sky spin
then go flat. It seems I should feel safe
here, though little things still confuse me.
It's hard to walk because the landscape
is distant and diminished, the streets and trees,
flimsy cardboard against a dirty white scrim.
Nothing moves. And then nothing stands still.
I am unable to read even the simplest texts
although I know to call them that. This morning
I woke up, not hopeful exactly, nor even
energetic, but I got out of bed by myself
and in the gray fog, I stood up.

Black Dog Goes to Art Colony

I like it here. I like it here. They do things in packs.
At night they pile together on the floor.
I lie down on the leather jackets and boots
and the skinny ties I sink my teeth into and shake.
Tonight, as usual, they are listening to someone talk.
I track the smells: linseed oil and mink oil,
bag balm, gasoline and tar, cigarettes.
Tall thin man smell, cologne and sweat.
Great big woman smell, plastic, powder and pastries.
That woman's still talking and now they've got a fire going,
smoke and pine and burning sap, and sulfur.
It's the fire makes them want to drowse and pet a dog.
I move to one side, then the other, to catch the petters
with soft hands, rough hands, shirt cuffs, sweaters.
The guy with the pickup truck takes me with him to the dump;
otherwise I don't have too many duties here.
I've found my place to settle among the brass studs
and the leather, the elbows and knees where
I'm waiting for the shoe to drop, for the talk to stop,
for them to whistle and clap for me,
to call my name, *good dog, good dog.*

Report from Here

Today, a sudden change in the weather.
At breakfast everyone was angry. Someone
sat in the wrong seat and someone else was jealous.
These two had words, and the rest of us stared
at our eggs. Nothing is more thrilling than passion,
the unlikely sparks an argument gives off,
someone with a book flipping through pages,
reading out passages with incomparable fire,
or the heat in the back seat of the car last night
on the snowy road, squeezed in beside a stranger.
Her voice had gone dry and her speech slurry
and soft, our thighs were touching and our faces
backlit every half mile by the passing houses.
Outside, cold wind like a heart attack,
and—nothing is more thrilling—our hushed voices,
where were we going? some vague, hasty plan,
both of us caught a little off balance by the speed
of what we almost undertook and then did not,
the door opening, others coming in with snow
on their boots, laughing, good night, good night . . .

Late Apology

Against the wind the leaves turned white.
We were never far from the sea.
All things are hung with light near water:
the tin roof of the cabin where we slept,
the pudgy scrub pine, red twist of manzanita.
I leaned against the wooden porch rail
and watched the surf's wrack slime the rocks.
Too much was said, or not enough, and it was late
when, toward dark, we drove through green
tunnels of eucalyptus to the redwoods.
What you did was mock me for my fear;
what I did not do was stop you.
We stood in the shadow of enormous trees
whose roots are knit together underground.
If one falls, another falls.
It was late and all things hung with light.

The Border

What's beyond the path
with the mounds of sticks and twigs,
the throaty pine cones and the slippery needles?
It's the gray scaly wall of the house
on rue de la Dysse in Montpeyroux.
It's the blue shutters.
No, not that, but the dark forest we almost
could not make out beyond the ovens
at the camp we found by trailing
tiny black and white signs
along the cobblestone highway.
Sometimes before the headaches start,
I see things. Often it's a pale yellow light
between branches of black trees. There must
be wind because the branches are moving.
It must be dusk because the light is fading;
winter, because there are no leaves.
There is no sound, but a thick humming
of something about to happen.
Just before the knife enters the nerve
above my left eye, I see the new refugees
running in their white headscarves
near the border. They are silent
and loaded down with bags, pulling children
behind them and looking both ways,
all ways, as they haul themselves
up the steep hill beside the paved road.

Foreign

Didn't say it right, said it dumb,
or some would say sweet, with an accent,
but wrong nonetheless. And so I sounded
inept and lost, and after a time,
even the kindest refuse to reward
merely the effort. It doesn't matter where
I come from, or what I do there.
Here I am wrong because I said it wrong,
startled or amused them, made them laugh,
gave them something to talk about
at dinner, the middle-aged woman
who came into the store and asked for . . .
the one who comes every day and still
hasn't said it right. You know,
the foreign one.

In Translation

Aalborg, Denmark, 1992

On both sides of the street the chestnut trees
have begun to bloom and their heavy flowers
are singular, like candles, each one
another thing I failed to do or did wrong.
I am not an unkind person.
Still, I have hurt people I love
and this sad realization hangs on my heart,
like the blossoms of the chestnut
the Danes call *kastanie,*
little white griefs,
sweet unintentioned wrongs.

Where

Car nous sommes où nous ne sommes pas.

—Pierre Jean-Jouve

It's a bit unclear because it's difficult
to decipher the French road signs and because
John keeps Anglicizing them so that
Lodève becomes *Low Dive,* 15 km from here.
It's the Languedoc and higher up,
the Cévennes, and everyone's language
has the low growl that reminds us of Montana
or maybe east Tennessee. So many
writers from the States have settled here
that the natives have started to resemble
talk show guests, quizzed about directions,
local wines, and pastries and baguettes.
In the evenings the women walk out of their houses
into the vineyards with their aprons still on,
or maybe a different apron, an outside apron,
not the one they cooked the meal in.
The men sit on the bench in the center of town
in black berets beside the angel's statue,
and they say, *Bonsoir, monsieur-dames.*
Sometimes we get confused and tell them
Bonjour! They are the bewildered citizens
gesticulating at us and the setting sun.
We are *va et vient,* where we are not,
or at some other time.

Literary

The first poems I read as if
they were printed on the wings of moths.
I had to read the same poem many times.
I understood nothing but was in love
with my own ignorance, which seemed
an uncertain field someone had ploughed up
without deciding to plant or leave fallow.
Or it was a flicker of yellow light
through a thick cover of maple leaves.
At first it was this,
then it became a more particularized confusion:
the white pot with the purple violet
nestled into furred foliage so coyly
it seemed almost to be flirting with me.
I learned to cook for more than hunger:
learned to add red peppers to offset the pink
tinge of the scampi, to marry herbs
with the essential body of pressed garlic,
and I had to learn to keep it simple.
In those days it was curiosity,
then later the oppositions drew me:
decorum and lawlessness,
indolence and rigor, or then, as now,
it was the secrecy I loved.
That, and appetite.

Self-Portrait

I was far outside the frame, beyond
the pale, lost in the margins, smudged
like a fingerprint and frankly, nervous
about holding my own. I knew what was coming:
you, toward me, your arms open,
preparing to wrap them around my neck
with the clear determination some people
bring to learning anthropology. I was not
about to be moved, to be swept off my feet
by your exotic bracelets. I'll admit
I sometimes incline toward
the minute particulars of a scene
but never have I been undone by a woman
on account of her accessories. Until now,
when I come into the picture, captivated
by black coral beads, the gold wire of an earring,
the rustle of red scarf against a neckline,
as this pull, this great tug at my heart,
forklifts me into the foreground
at the center of a photograph
of empty beach, empty that is except for
you, and pine and manzanita,
the silver rings and necklaces of white surf.

In the Midst of Our Happiness

We drive out to the orchards to walk among
the last of the apples and the D'Anjou pears.
At the end of the rows is a dark wood
where pale mosses spread across the nurse logs
like starched lace. Black branches against the sky
resemble the scratch of the crafter's mark
into pewter. We hold hands and look up and up,
in love with our barely forseeable futures.
Your hair is the only light place among
the wash of evergreens, and it burns the air.
All around us the countryside has gone
to wrack and ruin: small towns abandoned
and the fields uncut. How long did this take?
And how long for the devoted salmon
to make their way up the Nestucca to Beaver Creek
where they carve out the redds with their tails
and deposit their eggs in black bottom mud?
It has taken us a quarter of a century
to learn to lean against each other this way,
to stand together into darkness, when
we will, as we've grown accustomed,
lie down side by side on the forest floor.

What She Wrote

Sometimes nothing.

Sometimes an account of ocean
the accent or pitch of surf over tidepools
      that are like chafing dishes,
        the foamy sex of water in rivulets and crevices of driftwood
        moss agates the tides undress.

If something reminded her of something else,
like memory, like metaphor
she recorded it:

        the big pinecone from the fir tree which made her think
        of shiny stones, which made her think
        of the white muscats of Tuscany
        the grape scissors in her father's silver chest
        and, therefore, of her father,

who was like someone shadowed in evening light
when the sun peels down, ovarian and bloody at the horizon,
like pumpkins scooped out to make faces
with lighted eyes, dug up and planted on the porch.

Some days the water was gray-green and stormy
        dizzy with churn-up and scum, and then later
        the beach was littered with trunks of red cedar
            bull kelp, plastic shoes, jellyfish and kite string,
            tool boxes, food wrappers, dung.

Sometimes she wrote about a gray barn in West Virginia,
        or the cobbled streets of the Buda hills;
        the suns of yellow dahlias in the front yard in Ohio.

Sometimes she wrote down words that pleased her, nothing more:

> *Limpid. Land-locked.*
> *Cartography. Collander.*
> *Metal fatigue. Architecture,*

which reminded her of the feel of her softest shirt and of her mother,
the plaid viyella she wore like a uniform every day.

And almost every day she woke up rested.
She woke up rested almost every day.

My First Yiddish Poem

Yiddish [is the] only international language.
—Robin Becker

It was astonishingly easy to enter her *mishegoss*
and paste myself to it, the way the scabby moss
pastes itself to the tin roof, the way her body
pressed against mine and her whisper,
Don't talk, don't talk. We walked among
the odd Midwestern maples, box elder,
and my imagination was a little lazy,
somewhat lackluster from the hard winter's
filibuster of heavy snow. How did I find her,
a nervous Jew speaking Spanish to the waiter
in the Mexican restaurant on Hennepin Avenue,
then translating for me the French airbag warning
on the blue visor of her Fiat when she drove
me home? Was this a *tsimmes* or *tsuris?*

O my Talmudic scholar of the very-big-fuss,
that afternoon we sat on the manicured lawn
in the green Adirondack chairs—so Borscht Belt!
and yet so *goyishe!*—what were we doing
in this blue watery place where the last glacier
carved out bluffs, where Longfellow composed
his *Hiawatha* and they named a falls for it,
where wealthy Norwegians underwrote theatre,
sculpture, and Protestant humor? And why did you
run away? Perhaps you tired of me since, as you told me,
you're so much smarter. What was I? A *shmatte?*
It doesn't matter. I thought I had been waiting for you.
Listen. Buzz. Bees in the linden trees,
sweet wounds, *quelque chose.*

These Greens

    Inside the house, which is inside the boundaries of the farm,
which is inside the countryside beyond the highway and the town,
I sit on a red velveteen sofa among these objects: ruby glassware,
two brass dancing Shivas, several seated bodhisattvas, a green mask,
and one blue window. The pervasive smells are of must and damp,
in books and furniture; of incense; of cut grass and weeds; the hot
smell of dirt road dust kicked up; the wet, photosynthetic smell of
green, green, green.

> Say green across the meadow,
> to the margin of the forest where
> the dark emerges. The green
> in the forest is thicker than
> the green in the field. *Grandmother,*
> *are you right with Our Lord and Savior?*
> the child asks at supper.
> In this place it is difficult to talk
> without pain, words clot
> in the throat, arched and cankered,
> they stick and gag, viridian.
> Or they come in the diction
> of judgment and denial, crenelated
> into the silences the heat intersects.
> *Quiet is safer.* Lapses of consideration
> for others are amusing and everyone
> laughs. *That's just what you get!*
> There is plenty of room for a wandering
> attention. Some of us are slow.
> Some of us are thoughtful and some of us
> are feckless. Some of us are peeved.

Just before lunch I fell, sprawled across the big front room floor
as if pieces of me had suddenly acquired independent intelligences
and gone off on their own: my forearm scraped on who-knows-
what, spine crunched against the ceiling post that holds the house up,
shoulder to the sofa, one shoe off and one shoe on. Then I got
back up, plucky and determined and ate my lunch: tomato sandwich,
big yellow tomato shaped like an aubergine, like Andrew Jackson's
head. I ate slowly, but contentedly, in some pain, truth be told, but
nothing broken, nothing sprained. Now the afternoon is passing
faster than I thought it would, the sun already low across the
meadow, the green roof of the barn and the verdancy of open fields,
and I am typing in the throb of my mortality.

> Breast-high weeds. The saffron fringe at the edge
> of the forest is yellow tulle, or caterpillar scum.
> Something like drapery slings out of the branches
> of the tallest trees. Is it laundry or scenery?
>
> Yesterday I was swarmed by the bees I ran over
> with the lawnmower. Clearly they intended
> to kill me. I was stung eighteen times.
> Some of the stingers stuck on my face and
> on the back of my hand like tiny toothpicks.
>
> I made a paste of baking soda and water
> and covered all the stings until the thumping
> eased some. In the night, I woke hot and pained
> around my eyes where the swelling had not
> gone down. Today I am cooler but can
> feel it still. There is a poison in me.

The taffeta of chicory and joe-pye lavenders
and unravels. Brown hickory nuts are ripening,
green glass buttons on a blue suede jacket,
new jeans crackling as I walk. And on the far
hill above the four lane, a silk blouse,
one silk blouse, mouse-gray.

    The poem I read at the poetry conference was not about a penis. I
said "peninsula," but no one heard me. Later, David read his poem
about how, as a boy, he believed he would grow two penises since
women have two breasts. And then David One quoted David Two
and declared penises a "theme" for the gathering.

    I said "blue." I said "blue box" and "eternity." I said, when I
exhumed my father, his bones were intact only at the "peninsula" of
his spine and his clavicle. The rest of him was, as I expected,
just an assortment of bones and a gray damp spot where something
like his hair might have been twenty-five years ago. I said
"peninsula": cerebral cortex, cerebellum, a swarm of bees and no
box at all. If my father is not in the ground, in the box they
guaranteed would hold him just as he was on the day of his
burial for at least one hundred years, then where is my father?

I have collected the erotic and the breathless.
A cache of old papers, photographs,
pictures of bodies alive and sexual,
or dead, inside their satin-lined coffins.
Nothing has altered inside these boxes:
their contents remain *tableaux vivants.*
The photographs no longer hold my attention.
My own prose, if I may call it that,

from forty years ago is a stranger's, a child's.
Here is a letter to my mother in the hospital.
I was eight years old and didn't know she
was dying. I drew a picture for her of my parakeet.
Here is a stack of letters from Vietnam
and my old report cards. I was an indifferent
student who was going steady with a boy
who got drafted. He wrote me that we
should be married because we were just like
two peas in a pod. I study my drawing of
a bright green bird with a crown of vermilion
and claws like those of a bronze lion perched
heavily inside an iron cage. All of these pages
are fading and smudged on the edges with
the green pastel that comes off on my hands.

Inside the house, which is inside the boundaries of the farm, which is inside the countryside beyond the highway and the town, I sit on a red velveteen sofa among objects. Some of us are slow. Some of us are thoughtless and some of us are fertile. Some of us are peeved. Say green across the meadow to the margin of the forest. There is plenty of room for a wandering attention.

Notes

The title *Years That Answer* is taken from a sentence in Zora Neale Hurston's novel *Their Eyes Were Watching God:* "There are years that ask questions and years that answer."

The poem "In the Art of the Inuit" was originally titled "In the Art of the Eskimo," and the sections were based on reproductions of prints by artists of the West Baffin Island Eskimo Cooperative, Cape Dorset, Canada, in James Houston's 1967 book *Eskimo Art.* For this printing, I have changed "Eskimo" to "Inuit" as the name now preferred for the native peoples of Canada. The artists whose prints and titles are sources for the three sections of my poem printed here are: Sheowak, "Reflections in My Mind"; Lucy Qinnuayuak, "Owl with Young"; and Kenojuak Ashevak, "Complex of Birds."

 The poems "House and Graveyard, Rowlesburg, West Virginia, 1935," "Independence Day, Terra Alta, West Virginia, 1935," and "Mining Camp Residents, West Virginia, 1935," are based on photographs by Walker Evans. The titles of my poems are the same as Evans's titles for his photographs.

The title *A Space Filled with Moving* is taken from Gertrude Stein's *The Gradual Making of the Making of Americans:* "Think of anything, of cowboys, of movies, of detective stories, of anybody who goes anywhere or stays at home and is an American and you will realize that it is something strictly American to conceive of a space that is filled with moving, a space of time that is filled always filled with moving. . . ."

"Ontological" adapts the phrase "When you go looking for what is lost, everything is a sign," from Eudora Welty's story "The Wide Net."

"Closed Mill" quotes the motto on the Carnegie family coat

of arms, "Death to Privilege." The direct quote from Andrew Carnegie is attributed to him by Haniel Long in his book *Pittsburgh Memoranda*.

The poem "Late Apology" uses lines from two poems by Ann Stanford: "Too much was said or not enough" (from "The Self Betrayed") and "All things were hung with light" (from "A Birthday") in *The Descent*.

The following poems have dedications: "Caving" is dedicated to William Matthews (1942–1997); "Heart Fire" is in memory of Aaron Goodman (1962–1983) and is dedicated to Sharon Goodman; "Heart Labor" is dedicated to Tanya Agnostopoulou; "Beyond Even This" is dedicated to Lynn Emanuel; "Wild Berries" is dedicated to Louise McNeill (1911–1993); "The Only Angel" is dedicated to Jude Tallichet.

Acknowledgments

The poems included here are taken from three previous collections: *Years That Answer* (New York: Harper and Row, 1980); *Cold Comfort* (Pittsburgh: University of Pittsburgh Press, 1986, 1988); and *A Space Filled with Moving* (Pittsburgh: University of Pittsburgh Press, 1992). In addition, some of the poems from *Years That Answer* were first published in a limited edition chapbook, *The Great Horned Owl* (Riderwood, Md.: Icarus Press, 1979). Many of the poems in these earlier books were first published in magazines, and I thank the editors of the following magazines for permission to reprint them: *American Poetry Review, Backcountry, 5 A.M., Indiana Review, Northwest Review, Pennsylvania Review, Poetry East, Prairie Schooner, The Stone, 13th Moon,* and *Women's Review of Books.*

Some of the new poems here were published first in magazines, and I thank the editors for permission to reprint them: "Black Dog Remembers," "The Game," and "Black Dog Lies Down" in *The Marlboro Review;* "Late Apology" and "Self-Portrait" in *Third Coast;* "Report from Here" in the *Ohio Review;* "The Border" and "In Translation" in *Great River Review;* and "Foreign" and "My First Yiddish Poem" in *Women's Review of Books.*

I am grateful for 1984 and 1990 fellowships from the National Endowment for the Arts and for fellowships from the Ohio Arts Council, the Pennsylvania Council on the Arts, and the West Virginia Arts and Humanities Commission. The Research Council of Kent State University has awarded me several grants which provided essential time for writing. I also thank the MacDowell Colony in Peterborough, New Hampshire, and the Anderson Center for Interdisciplinary Studies in Red Wing, Minnesota, where many of these poems were written.

For necessary support and guidance at crucial points during the twenty-five years of writing these poems I am deeply grateful to the following people: Gwendolyn Brooks, Jane Cooper, Winston Fuller, Maxine Kumin, William Matthews (in memoriam), Irene McKinney, Louise McNeill (in memoriam), Anna Mitgutsch, Ed Ochester, Tillie Olsen, Alicia Ostriker, Gerald Stern, and Judith Stitzel. For careful readings of the recent poems and for help with the selections for this book I am grateful to Jan Beatty, Robin Becker, David Hassler, Julia Kasdorf, Maxine Scates, Robyn Selman, and as always, The Group: Pat Dobler, Lynn Emanuel, and Judith Vollmer.

MAGGIE ANDERSON is the author of three previous collections of poetry, *Years That Answer, Cold Comfort,* and *A Space Filled with Moving,* editor of *Hill Daughter: New and Selected Poems of Louise McNeill,* and co-editor of *A Gathering of Poets* and *Learning by Heart: Contemporary American Poetry about School.* Maggie Anderson has received awards from the National Endowment for the Arts, the Ohio Arts Council, the Pennsylvania Council on the Arts, and the MacDowell Colony. She teaches creative writing at Kent State University, where she directs the Wick Poetry Program and edits the Wick Poetry Series, published by the Kent State University Press.